Off We Go for a Haircut

Avril Webster
Illustrated by David Ryley

Woodbine House 2011

Dedication

This series of books is dedicated to Stephen and Christia,
the children who inspired its creation.

Acknowledgements

- I would like to thank David Ryley, the artist for the series, whose talent, compassion, and sense of humor are evident in all the illustrations.

- I would also like to thank Stephen's speech & language therapist, his teachers, and the mothers of his classmates for their contributions to these books.

First American edition published in 2011 by Woodbine House, Inc., 6510 Bells Mill Rd., Bethesda, MD 20817. 800-843-7323. www.woodbinehouse.com. All rights reserved under International and Pan-American copyright conventions.

Library of Congress Cataloging-in-Publication Data

Webster, Avril.
  Off we go for a haircut / Avril Webster ; illustrated by David Ryley. -- 1st American ed.
      p. cm. -- (Off we go)
  ISBN 978-1-60613-019-3
  1. Haircutting--Juvenile literature. I. Ryley, David. II. Title.
  TT970.W43 2011
  646.7'24--dc22

                                                                                                    2010045381

Printed in the United States of America

10   9   8   7   6   5   4   3   2   1

I am going to get my hair cut.

"Hello!" I tell the person behind the desk. "I'm here."

I sit and wait for my turn. I look at a magazine.

I sit very still and let the hairdresser cut my hair.
The scissors don't hurt.

Look, it's my friend! The hairdresser uses clippers to cut his hair. The clippers make a funny sound but they don't hurt either.

The hairdresser dries my hair with a hairdryer. It blows warm air and makes a loud noise. It will be over soon.

The hairdresser puts hair spray in my hair.
I look nice!

The hairdresser takes off the cape.
Look at all the hair on the floor!

I pay for my haircut.

"Bye bye, thank you. See you next time."